T0062306

What Farmers Need to Know

Joe Rhatigan

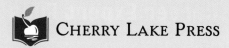

CHERRY LAKE PRESS

Published in the United States of America by Cherry Lake Publishing Group
Ann Arbor, Michigan
www.cherrylakepublishing.com

Reading Adviser: Beth Walker Gambro, MS, Ed., Reading Consultant, Yorkville, IL

Photo Credits: © La Famiglia/Shutterstock, cover, 1; © StockMediaSeller/Shutterstock, 5; © Carl Ning/Shutterstock, 7;
© yelantsevv/Shutterstock, 8; © Nicola Pulham/Shutterstock, 9; © Jasmine Sahin/Shutterstock, 11; © Dejan Dundjerski/
Shutterstock, 13; © Olga Geo/Shutterstock, 14; © Elena Masiutkina/Shutterstock, 15; © Martin Helgemeir/Shutterstock,
16; © Juice Verve/Shutterstock, 19; © Valentin Valkov/Shutterstock, 20; © alexmisu/Shutterstock, 21; © Juice Verve/
Shutterstock, 23; © ancoay/Shutterstock, 24; © S1001/Shutterstock, 25; © l i g h t p o e t/Shutterstock, 27;
© l i g h t p o e t/Shutterstock, 28; © Thanakorn.P/Shutterstock, 29

Cherry Lake Press is an imprint of Cherry Lake Publishing Group.

Library of Congress Cataloging-in-Publication Data

Names: Rhatigan, Joe, author.
Title: What farmers need to know / written by Joe Rhatigan.
Description: Ann Arbor, Michigan : Cherry Lake Publishing, [2024] | Series: Career expert files | Includes bibliographical
    references and index. | Audience: Grades 4-6 | Summary: "Farmers need to have the expert knowledge, skills, and
    tools to keep the world fed. The Career Expert Files series covers professionals who are experts in their fields. These
    career experts know things we never thought they'd need to know, but we're glad they do"— Provided by publisher.
Identifiers: LCCN 2023035042 | ISBN 9781668939130 (paperback) | ISBN 9781668938096 (hardcover) |
    ISBN 9781668940471 (ebook) | ISBN 9781668941829 (pdf)
Subjects: LCSH: Farmers—Juvenile literature. | Agriculture—Vocational guidance—Juvenile literature.
Classification: LCC S519 .R47 2024 | DDC 635.023—dc23/eng/20230831
LC record available at https://lccn.loc.gov/2023035042

Cherry Lake Publishing Group would like to acknowledge the work of the Partnership for 21st Century Learning,
a Network of Battelle for Kids. Please visit Battelle for Kids online for more information.

Printed in the United States of America

Note from publisher: Websites change regularly, and their future contents are outside of our control.
Supervise children when conducting any recommended online searches for extended learning opportunities.

Joe Rhatigan lives in Western North Carolina with his family and Jumbo Shrimp, a cat,
and Rooster, a dog. He writes, edits, reads, buys, and adores books.

CONTENTS

In the Know

Every career you can imagine has one thing in common. It takes an expert. Career experts need to know more about how to do a specific job than other people do. That's how everyone from plumbers to rocket scientists get their jobs done.

Sometimes it takes years of college study to learn what they need to know. Other times, people learn by working alongside someone who is already a career expert. No matter how they learn, it takes a career expert to do any job well.

Take farmers, for instance. These professionals feed the world. They know how to cultivate and care for crops and **livestock** that people eat to survive. They know about soil and weather conditions. They know how to grow different foods and how to keep them watered. And so much more!

Does the idea of working the land appeal to you? Do you like working outdoors to get big jobs done? Would you like to grow a career as a farmer? Here are some things you need to know.

Farmers Are Good at:

- Problem-solving
- Long-term planning
- Respecting the land
- Taking care of living things

CHAPTER 1

Farmers Know... How to Grow Good Food

Crops are plants that are grown and **harvested** by farmers. Some are for humans to eat. These include foods like spinach, broccoli, and watermelon. Corn is grown both for humans and animals. Barley, oats, and sorghum are also used for livestock food. Livestock are animals used for their milk, wool, or meat. Crop fibers can be used to make fabric. The fabric is used for socks, shirts, and other clothing.

Agriculture, or farming, is the science of growing crops. It's also the science of raising animals for food. Humans have been farming for 12,000 years. It is the foundation of civilization. Today, farms grow the fruits and vegetables we eat. They grow herbs used for medicines. They grow crops for fibers used in clothing. Farmers also raise **domesticated** animals for milk, eggs, and meat.

Terraced rice paddies have been used for farming in Asia for anywhere from about 650 to 740 years.

Commercial farms do everything on a large scale. About 20 states are currently home to commercial tomato farms. About $1 billion worth of tomatoes were harvested in 2020 in the United States.

Farming is a business. Some large commercial farms are owned by corporations. Most farms are family owned. Those farmers oversee everything from seeds to harvest. Like all businesses, they want to make a profit.

Successful farmers learn which plants to grow in which season. They figure out how to maximize their land. They fit as many plants as possible. They must keep the soil healthy. Then it can be used for years to come.

THE FOUNDATION OF CIVILIZATION

The last ice age on Earth ended around 10,000 years ago. Humans at this time largely hunted for meat to eat. They also foraged for plants and nuts. This system worked for small groups of people. But the climate warmed. Humans came up with new ideas and technologies. These technologies included irrigation systems. They started farming. Suddenly, all the food needed was in one place. As a result, the population increased. People started living in bigger and bigger communities, such as villages and cities. From here, societies and cultures formed. Civilization was born.

Farmers are also responsible for buying and caring for equipment. Most farming equipment is very expensive. Using it correctly can make farming easier and more effective. Farmers hire workers and keep track of the money. The same is true for **ranchers**. They raise and care for cattle, poultry, pigs, sheep, and goats.

Farming also involves selling products. Some farmers might sell directly to people at farmer's markets. They may sell through community-supported agriculture (CSAs). CSAs sell **shares** to families each year. The shares provide these families with weekly boxes of produce. CSAs have become popular as people realize their value. With CSAs, people get farm-to-table food choices. Some farmers also sell to food processors or **distributors**. Food processors and distributors then sell it to stores.

All of this work takes someone who knows plants and animals. This person also needs to be good at making decisions. *When is the best time to buy new equipment? What crops will customers most want next year? How will the weather impact my crops?* These are just a few of the questions a farmer asks. They consider these questions before planting even one seed.

With CSAs, farmers can go directly to their consumers. CSAs help create a stronger community tie to local farms.

The United States has more than 2 million farms. Small farms produce almost one-third of the world's food. The world's population is expected to hit 9 billion people within 30 years. So farmers need to find even smarter ways to farm. Their knowledge and hard work will keep our stomachs full. Using the latest science and technology will keep people fed. The world will always need farmers.

CHAPTER 2

Farmers Know... How to Make a Living from the Land

A farmer looks out over her fields. The soil has been **tilled** and **furrowed** and is ready for planting. The planter is at the edge of the field. It is ready to drop seeds into the ground. It's an exciting time for farmers. A lot of preparation helps grow these seeds into plants.

There are six types of soil for farming. They are sand, clay, silt, chalk, peat, and loam. Farmers run tests on soil. They make sure it has the right nutrients.

Different crops need different types of soil. For example, sandy soil warms up quickly after winter. It is great for early-season plants. Early-season plants include strawberries and lettuce. Potatoes and broccoli prefer heavy clay soil. It holds moisture that these plants need.

If the soil is healthy, plants growing from the soil will be healthier. Different plants thrive in different kinds of soil.

Planting something at the wrong time could ruin a crop. That's why farmers know the area's average temperature. They know when the last freeze usually occurs. They know about rainfall patterns. They know the amount of sunlight their fields receive. They are aware of how extreme the weather can get.

Water is essential to farmers. That's why farmers are careful to manage their water resources. They plan when and how to water their crops.

Anywhere between 20 and 40 percent of the world's crops are lost. They are lost to pests and diseases every year. Farmers know how to control pests using **pesticides**. They also use natural techniques. Most pesticides are chemicals applied to plants to repel bugs. Pesticides may kill the bad bugs. But they also kill the good ones—like bees. Pests can also grow resistant to certain pesticides.

Phytophthora Infestans (otherwise known as late blight) is a disease that attacks potatoes and tomatoes.

Free-range meats are from animals that were not caged as they were being raised.

Organic farms avoid using human-made **fertilizers** and pesticides. They use natural pesticides made from things found in nature. Organic farming requires a bit more work and land. Many people are happy to pay extra for organic foods.

Farmers need to know what certain types of animals need. These farmers provide food, water, grooming, and a safe environment. These animals need room to roam. Farmers also protect their animals from disease with vaccinations. Free-range animals are allowed to live more naturally. They are said by some to produce healthier food.

THINKING OUTSIDE THE BOX

Sometimes farmers think of new ideas for making money. Some sell produce directly to customers at farmer's markets. This removes the need to transport the veggies to stores. At these markets, farmers set up tables or booths with their food.

Some farmers sell shares of their crops. Each shareholder gets a box of fresh produce each week.

Fruit farmers sometimes let their customers pick their own fruit. Farms where families can pick berries or apples are popular. Sometimes there are hayrides involved!

Some farms go all out with fall festivals. Here, people come to enjoy games, corn, mazes, and pumpkins. Some invite the public to celebrate winter holidays. They may have decorations, hot cocoa, and s'mores. Farms can also be turned into educational places. Then kids can learn how to farm over the summer. Don't forget about goat yoga. Yes, it's a real thing!

CHAPTER 3

Farmers Know... The Tools of the Trade

Imagine you have a small garden in your backyard. You use a tiller to turn over the soil. You use it to break up clumps. This prepares soil for planting. With a shovel, you dig some holes. You plant the seeds with your hands. You water the seeds with a garden hose or a watering can. Farmers must do the same things. But they do these things on a much larger scale. They need bigger tools.

The most common farm vehicle is a tractor. They come in many sizes. They can plow, till the soil, and plant. They can even pull other vehicles and transport livestock. Driverless tractors are sometimes used on bigger farms.

Tractors come in all sorts of different shapes and sizes.
They have many different uses.

Tilling the soil helps get the soil ready for planting.

To get soil ready, farmers use a couple of different tools. Tractors drag plows through the field to prepare soil. Plows look like giant rakes. They have metal disks that dig into the soil.

A tractor pulls the planter. This machine holds the seeds. It releases them at the proper depth in rows. A sprayer is used to apply fertilizer and pesticides.

Farmers often use all-terrain vehicles (ATVs). They use them to inspect crops, fences, irrigation systems, and livestock. There is a lot of ground to cover. Farmers need to make the most of their time.

A combine harvester is used for harvesting grain crops. These crops include plants like wheat, corn, and rice. The combine harvester cuts the crops. It then separates the grains from the stalks. Finally, it collects them.

A hay baler bundles dried grass for livestock feed.

Farmers use hand tools or their hands to harvest certain crops. Hand-harvested crops include fruit from trees, garlic, and vanilla.

WATER ME

Most farms are too big to water with a hose. Farmers use a variety of techniques for watering. Water can be piped to each plant. Crops may be watered through pipes with holes in them. These pipes drip water to each plant. Sprinklers on wheeled towers are sometimes used on flat fields. Many of these systems are automated. This way, farmers can count on the job getting done right.

CHAPTER 4

Farmers Know... How to Farm Safely

Farming involves a lot of complicated machinery. Farmers keep safety front and center at all times. Gloves, boots, goggles, and proper headgear are a must.

Ergonomics is the study of people in their working environment. The goal is to make sure that the work environment is safe. It should be free of discomfort and risk of injury. For farmers, that means knowing how to lift heavy objects properly. It also means drinking plenty of water on hot days. It means taking breaks and using the proper tools for each job. Farmers must take care of themselves. Then they can take good care of their farms.

Knowing how to interact with animals is also an important part of farm safety.

If farm equipment isn't properly maintained,
it could be dangerous!

Farmers need to know how to properly use their equipment. It's not enough to make sure your heavy machinery works. Farmers need to inspect and maintain farm equipment regularly. This reduces the chance of injury. Are all the guards and shields needed in place? Does the chainsaw you're using to cut a tree limb have sharpened blades? Poorly maintained equipment can cause injuries.

ANIMALS ON A FARM

Farmers also need to keep their animals safe! Did you know that chickens lay up to 350 eggs a year? So do ducks. Chickens also provide meat and feathers. Their droppings are used as fertilizer. Cows are raised not only for their milk and meat. They're also raised for creating leather products. These products include belts, shoes, and luggage. Dogs protect the farm from animal intruders. But so can parrots! The bird's sounds can alert a farmer to predators. There are many ways farm animals are important.

CHAPTER 5

Farmers Know... How to Find the Job They Want

There are other farmers outside of crop or livestock farmers. There are other interesting types of farming. For instance, organic farming uses natural ways to grow crops. It uses natural ways to raise animals. It doesn't use chemical pesticides and fertilizers.

Sustainable farming focuses on helping the soil stay healthy. Sustainable farmers plant several different crops over the seasons. This is instead of just one crop. This is good for the environment and the soil.

Organic farms raise animals naturally, without using antibiotics or growth hormones.

Aquaculture is another type of farming. Instead of crops, farmers raise fish or shellfish in water.

County extension agents work in communities. They answer questions about gardening, agriculture, and pest control. They run special events and projects to promote local agriculture. They may also sponsor 4-H clubs to interest young people in agricultural activities.

TRUE OR FALSE

Farmers are uneducated, old-fashioned, and stuck in their ways.

Answer: False. False. And false! This is a myth that is wrong on so many levels. Books, movies, and TV shows sometimes present farmers as "country bumpkins." These farmers may be surrounded by cutesy farm animals. The reality is that it takes knowledge to farm successfully. Farmers must stay on top of fast-changing technology. They need to know their science. They must use business management tools needed to run a farm. Many farmers have college degrees. Whether or not a farmer has a degree, you can bet they are an expert in their field.

Agronomists are also known as crop scientists. They are experts in the science of agriculture.

Agronomists are scientists who are interested in soil health. They help farmers decide which crops to grow. They help them choose what to feed their plants. They help them decide how to safely eradicate pests. Some work for the government or in research labs.

Do you love managing lots of people? You can become a farm manager. They oversee the day-to-day operations

Activity

Stop, Think, and Write

Can you imagine a world without farmers? What would we eat?

Get a separate sheet of paper. On one side, answer these questions:

- *How do farmers make the world a better place?*
- *If you were a farmer, what would you want to grow?*
- *Where would you grow your crops?*

On the other side of the paper:

- *Draw a picture of you as a farmer growing your favorite crop.*

Things to Do If You Want to Be a Farmer

Many people get the experience they need to become a farmer because it's what their parents, grandparents, or siblings do. In other words, they are growing up on a farm! But even if the sound of roosters crowing doesn't wake you up each morning before dawn, you can still get farming experience right now.

NOW

- Find out if any farms near you offer tours or family day activities.
- See if your school district has a Future Farmers of America (FFA) club you can join.
- Get involved in your local 4-H program. It stands for Head, Heart, Hands, and Health.
- Try growing your own plants out in the yard or on a windowsill—just give your green thumb a workout.

LATER

- Look into apprenticeship or internship opportunities to work at a farm.
- Take any agriculture classes that your high school offers.
- Check out classes offered by the United States Department of Agriculture (USDA).
- Consider pursuing a college degree in agriculture, biology, animal husbandry, or sustainable horticulture.

Learn More

Books

Baliga, Vikram. *Plants to the Rescue.* New York, NY: Neon Squid, 2023.

Castaldo, Nancy. *The Farm that Feeds Us: A Year in the Life of an Organic Farm.* London, UK: words & pictures, 2020.

Henzel, Cynthia Kennedy. *Jobs in Agriculture.* North Mankato, MN: ABDO, 2023.

Reeves, Diane Lindsey. *World of Work: Food and Natural Resources.* Ann Arbor, MI: Cherry Lake, 2017.

On the Web

With an adult, learn more online with these suggested searches.

4-H Clubs

Community Gardens

Future Farmers of America (FFA) Clubs

Urban Farming

Glossary

distributors (dih-STRIH-byoo-tuhrz) businesses that move goods to where they are needed

domesticated (duh-MEH-stih-kay-tuhd) animals that have adapted to live with people as pets or on a farm

fertilizers (FUHR-tuh-liye-zuhrz) substances added to the soil or sprayed on plants to keep them nourished

foraged (FOHR-ijd) searched for food or supplies

furrowed (FUHR-ohd) formed a long, narrow ditch in the soil for planting seeds

harvested (HAR-vuhst-ed) gathered in a crop

irrigation (ear-uh-GAY-shuhn) adding water to farm fields

livestock (LIYV-stahk) domestic animals kept by people for meat, milk, leather, or wool

pesticides (PEH-stuh-siydz) substances used to control or kill insects and other pests

ranchers (RAN-chuhrz) farmers who raise livestock for meat

shares (SHAIRZ) part ownership in a business

tilled (TILD) prepared the soil for planting

Index